Learn About
SATURN!

BY NATALIE HUMPHREY

Enslow
PUBLISHING

DISCOVER!

Please visit our website, www.enslow.com. For a free color catalog of all our high-quality books, call toll free 1-800-398-2504 or fax 1-877-980-4454.

Cataloging-in-Publication Data

Names: Humphrey, Natalie.
Title: Learn about Saturn! / Natalie Humphrey.
Description: New York : Enslow Publishing, 2024. | Series: Planets in our solar system | Includes index.
Identifiers: ISBN 9781978533646 (pbk.) | ISBN 9781978533653 (library bound) | ISBN 9781978533660 (ebook)
Subjects: LCSH: Saturn (Planet)–Juvenile literature.
Classification: LCC QB671.H857 2024 | DDC 523.46–dc23

Portions of this work were originally authored by Daisy Allyn and published as *Saturn: The Ringed Planet*. All new material in this edition authored by Natalie Humphrey.

Published in 2024 by
Enslow Publishing
2544 Clinton Street
Buffalo, NY 14224

Designer: Andrea Davison-Bartolotta
Editor: Natalie Humphrey

Photo credits: Cover (Saturn), p. 1 (Saturn) MarcelClemens/Shutterstock.com; cover (top), p. 1 (top), series art (backgrounds) Jurik Peter/Shutterstock.com; series art (lens flare) andruxevich/Shutterstock.com; p. 4 Natee Jitthammachai/Shutterstock.com; p. 5 3000ad/Shutterstock.com; p. 7 Alhovik/Shutterstock.com; p. 9 joshimerbin/Shutterstock.com; p. 10 (bath tub) Pratchaya.Lee/Shutterstock.com; p. 10 (saturn) Pike-28/Shutterstock.com; pp. 11, 15 Vadim Sadovski/Shutterstock.com; p. 13 NASA/JPL/Space Science Institute; p. 17 Media Whale Stock/Shutterstock.com; p. 19 Beyond Space/Shutterstock.com; p. 21 NASA/JPL-Caltech.

CPSIA compliance information: Batch #CS24ENS: For further information contact Enslow Publishing, at 1-800-398-2504.

Find us on

CONTENTS

Boldface words appear in Words to Know.

Ringed
PLANET

Have you ever heard of a planet with rings around it? You might be thinking of Saturn! Saturn has some of the biggest rings in the **solar system**. Saturn's rings are so big, you can see them clearly through a **telescope**!

SATURN

Saturn usually orbits at around 886 million miles (1.4 billion km) from the sun.

A Long YEAR

Saturn has a long **orbit**. It takes Saturn around 29 Earth years to travel around the sun once! One day on Saturn is much shorter than it is on Earth, though. It only takes Saturn about 10.7 Earth hours to spin completely around.

Saturn moves at around 22,000 miles (35,000 km) per hour.

Mercury

Venus

Earth

Mars

Jupiter

Saturn

Uranus

Neptune

Gas GIANT

Saturn is a gas giant. Most of Saturn is made up of liquid **hydrogen** and **helium**. Saturn's center, or core, is likely hot and rocky. Saturn is the second-largest planet in our solar system. The only planet that is larger is Jupiter!

JUPITER

SATURN

Although Saturn is made of the same matter as the sun, it could never be a star because it doesn't have enough **mass**.

Saturn may be a giant planet, but scientists believe it's not very **dense**. In fact, water is more dense than Saturn. That means if we had a bathtub that was big enough to fit all of Saturn, Saturn would likely float!

IMAGINE THIS!

Saturn is the lightest planet in the solar system.

Saturn's
RINGS

Saturn's rings are one of its most famous features! Saturn's rings are made out of mostly ice. There are also chunks of rock and dust in Saturn's rings. These chunks orbit Saturn just like Saturn orbits the sun.

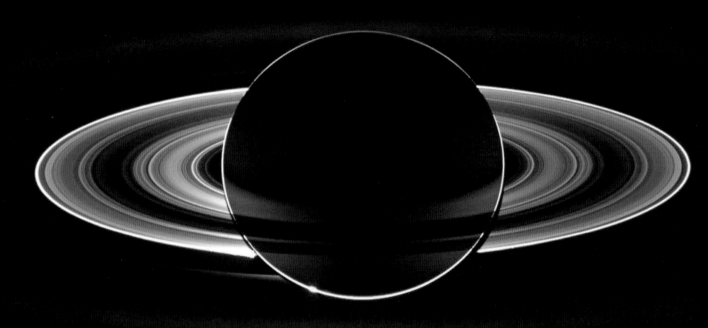

Saturn has seven
groups of rings.

Saturn's
MOONS

Saturn has a lot of moons. Some are very big, and some are very small. Saturn's smallest known moon is not even large enough to hold a round shape. Saturn's largest moon is Titan. Titan is the second-largest moon in the solar system.

SOME OF SATURN'S MOONS

TITAN   RHEA   IAPETUS

DIONE   TETHYS   ENCELADUS

Titan is even bigger than the planet Mercury!

Could There BE LIFE?

Saturn doesn't have the right **environment** for life like us to live. But some of Saturn's moons might! Two of Saturn's moons, Titan and Enceladus, have one very important thing: water. These moons have oceans under their outer coating.

TITAN

Even though Titan
has water, life hasn't
been found on it.

No one has ever walked on Saturn, but scientists can still study it! Not only can Saturn be seen through telescopes on Earth, but scientists have also sent **probes** to study it. One **spacecraft**, as part of a study, crashed into Saturn!

VOYAGER
SPACE PROBE

The Voyager space probes passed Saturn in 1980 and 1981.

In 1997, NASA sent off the Cassini-Huygens spacecraft. This spacecraft had one **mission**: explore Saturn! Cassini traveled 4.9 billion miles (7.9 billion km) total and orbited Saturn 294 times. By the end of its mission, Cassini had taken more than 450,000 pictures of Saturn!

CASSINI-HUYGENS SPACECRAFT

Scientists still haven't discovered everything there is to know about Saturn.

WORDS TO KNOW

dense: Packed very closely together.

environment: The conditions that surround a living thing and affect the way it lives.

helium: One of the most common gases in our solar system.

hydrogen: A common gas.

mass: The amount of matter in an object.

mission: A task or job a group must perform.

orbit: To travel in a circle or oval around something.

probe: An unmanned spaceship.

solar system: The sun and all the space objects that orbit it, including the planets and their moons.

spacecraft: A human-made object sent into space for exploration or research.

telescope: A tool that makes faraway objects look bigger and closer.

FOR MORE INFORMATION

BOOKS

Mitchell, K. S. *The Gas Giants: Jupiter, Saturn, Uranus, and Neptune*. San Diego, CA: BrightPoint Press, 2023.

Storm, Marysa. *Saturn*. Mankato, MN: 2023

WEBSITES

NASA Space Place
spaceplace.nasa.gov/all-about-saturn/en/
Learn more interesting facts from the people exploring Saturn at NASA!

National Geographic Kids
kids.nationalgeographic.com/space/article/mission-to-saturn
Check out more information, fun videos, and pictures of Saturn.

INDEX